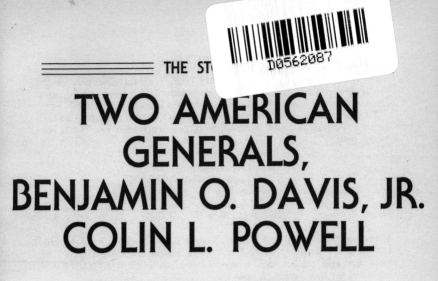

THE ST... **D0562087**

TWO AMERICAN GENERALS, BENJAMIN O. DAVIS, JR. COLIN L. POWELL

BY KATHERINE APPLEGATE

A YEARLING BOOK

ABOUT THIS BOOK

The events described in this book are true. They have been carefully researched and excerpted from authentic autobiographies, writings, and commentaries. No part of this biography has been fictionalized.

To learn more about General Benjamin O. Davis, Jr., and General Colin L. Powell, ask your librarian to recommend other fine books you might read.

Published by
Dell Publishing
a division of
Bantam Doubleday Dell Publishing Group, Inc.
666 Fifth Avenue
New York, New York 10103

Cover Photo Credits:
Aircraft carrier: PH1 Scott Allen/Dept. of Defense
Davis and Powell: Craig Herndon/Washington Post
Davis on plane: The New York Public Library/The Schomburg Center for Research and Black Culture
Powell in uniform: AP/Wide World Photos

ISBN: 0-440-40595-5

Published by arrangement with Parachute Press, Inc.
Printed in the United States of America
January 1992
10 9 8 7 6 5 4 3 2 1
OPM

Contents

To Michael,
with thanks for all his help

The author wishes to thank Benjamin O. Davis, Jr., whose autobiography, *Benjamin O. Davis, Jr., American*, was of great assistance in writing this book.

Introduction

Ever since the very first battles of the Revolutionary War, black Americans and white Americans have fought courageously to defend their country. But they haven't always fought together as equals. For most of American history, the military was segregated, which meant that blacks and whites were separated into different groups. They were fighting the same enemies, but the two races weren't allowed to serve together. Many people believed that blacks weren't intelligent enough or brave enough for combat.

When Benjamin O. Davis, Jr., joined the military, he set out to prove those people wrong. It wasn't easy. He was the first black man in this century ever to attend the U.S. Military Academy at West Point, where students learn to become officers. Benjamin attended West Point from 1932–1936, but his classmates refused to accept him as their equal, simply because he was black. They punished him in the worst way they knew—they refused even to speak to him for the entire four years he was there. Then, when he graduated, Benjamin was told to give up his dream of becoming a fighter pilot. Blacks weren't allowed to fly planes for the military.

But World War II changed all that. Military leaders needed more pilots, and at last they were willing to give blacks a chance. Benjamin became the leader of the first black fighter pilot squadron in American history. Their stunning record in the war proved once and for all that blacks could play an important role in the military. All they had needed was the chance to prove themselves.

Benjamin Davis's bravery and determination made it easier for other blacks who followed in his footsteps—men like Colin Powell. Colin was just a boy when Benjamin Davis was fighting in the skies overseas. But he would grow up to become the first black in history to be Chairman of the Joint Chiefs of Staff—America's highest-ranking military officer. As Chairman, General Powell helped direct the American military to an impressive victory in the Persian Gulf War.

This is the story of two American military

heroes, men who served their country with courage and honor. As they fought for their country, they also fought another battle—the battle for the rights of blacks in the military.

General
Benjamin O. Davis, Jr.

Night of Terror

Benjamin stared out the window. The street in front of his house was empty. His neighborhood looked dark and deserted. A strange stillness hung in the air.

Benjamin's father came into the room. He was dressed in his crisp white Army uniform, one he wore only on special occasions. Benjamin always felt proud when he saw his father wearing it. But tonight he was feeling something else—fear. Real, deep-down fear.

Lieutenant Colonel Benjamin Davis joined his son at the window. Outside, every house was dark. Not a single light was on. It looked as though all of Tuskegee, Alabama, had been abandoned.

Benjamin looked down the street and saw flickering torches. It was the Ku Klux Klan, getting ready to march.

Benjamin was only ten years old, but he already knew about *them*. He knew because he was black, and the Klan hated anyone who was black. In the 1920s, when he was growing up, the Klan terrorized and murdered black people all across the South.

The Klan was holding a march that night because a new hospital for black veterans had just been built nearby. Klansmen wanted all the doctors and nurses at the hospital to be white, even though the patients were black. They wanted whites to have all the good jobs.

The black people in Benjamin's neighborhood had been warned to stay in their houses during the Klan march. But Colonel Davis reached for the light switch. The porch outside was flooded with light. Then he opened the door and started out.

Benjamin swallowed hard. He and his father would be the only black people in sight when the Klan marched by. What would the Klansmen do when they saw his family?

Benjamin thought of all the signs he had seen saying "Colored" and "Whites Only." He thought of the horrible, hurtful names that white children sometimes called black children. Most of all he thought of the burnings and beatings and hangings he'd heard about ever since he could remember.

But—if his father could do it, he could, too. He and Lieutenant Colonel Davis stepped out into the cool night air. And the rest of the family joined them.

A large mob of men carrying flaming torches was marching down the street. They wore long white sheets and pointed white hats. Their eyes barely showed through holes cut in the white cloth, but Benjamin knew those eyes were filled with hate.

The family stood quietly as the Klansmen drew closer and closer. Colonel Davis looked straight ahead, his head held high. His brass buttons and his medals gleamed in the bright porch light. Benjamin held his head high, too.

The Klansmen neared them. Would they attack? As the first of them passed, they turned to stare at the Davis family. Benjamin could feel their hatred. He could smell the smoke of their burning torches. But he was determined to be as brave as his father.

The Klansmen kept marching.

It seemed to take forever for them to pass by, but finally they were gone. Their torches still glowed in the distance. But the Davis family's porch light glowed just as brightly.

Into the Sky

The night of the Klan wasn't Benjamin's first experience with racism. Unfortunately, it wouldn't be his last, either.

Benjamin O. Davis, Jr., was born on December 18, 1912. It was a time when black people were separated from white people by a system called *segregation*. Benjamin and his family weren't allowed to live in white neighborhoods. They couldn't eat in white restaurants or stay in white hotels. Wherever they went, they had to use restrooms and drinking fountains marked "Colored."

In the Army, black soldiers were segregated from white ones. They were almost never put in fighting units—instead they were given kitchen work and clean-up duty. Black officers like Benjamin's father were never allowed to command white soldiers. They were sent to one of the few "colored" Army posts.

Still, Benjamin's father was devoted to the

Army. No matter what assignment he was given, he worked hard at it. Most of the white people he worked with were very prejudiced. They thought blacks weren't as intelligent or as skilled as whites. But Benjamin's father always reminded him that he was just as good as anyone else. And he told his son to treat other people the way he would want to be treated himself.

When Benjamin was three years old, his mother died after giving birth to his little sister Elnora. Benjamin had loved her very much, and her death left him terribly unhappy.

Soon afterward, his father received a new assignment. Lieutenant Colonel Davis was being sent to work overseas at an Army post in the Philippine Islands. Benjamin's father explained to him and his sisters that children weren't allowed at the base. They would have to stay behind.

Benjamin's grandparents in Washington, D.C., agreed to care for him and his two sisters—baby Elnora, and Olive, who was seven years older than he. But Benjamin didn't like living there. His grandfather was very strict. When he came home from work all the children had to be very quiet while he sat in his big chair and read the newspaper. They had the feeling that their grandfather didn't like them or want them there.

Fortunately, a number of aunts and uncles lived just a block away. Benjamin was their favorite nephew, and he was always welcome. His Aunt Lyd taught him how to make root beer. His Uncle Ernest took him for long streetcar rides around Washington. And he got Benjamin his very first job, delivering newspapers for the *Evening Star*.

Often Uncle Ernest would take him out to the country to visit another uncle named Louis, who owned a farm. Benjamin loved visiting with his uncle and playing with his cousins. There were animals on the farm—horses, cows, pigs, and a Mexican burro named Tipperary. Benjamin enjoyed riding him a lot. But Tipperary may not have enjoyed it quite as much— once he even bit Benjamin. According to the family story, Benjamin bit the burro right back!

While Benjamin's father was in the Philippines, he began writing to a friend of the family named Sadie Overton, an English professor in Washington. Two years later, on Christmas Eve, 1919, seven-year-old Benjamin got the present of his dreams. Sadie Overton traveled all the way to the Philippines and married his father.

11

When Benjamin was eight, Lieutenant Colonel Davis and Sadie returned to the United States. Benjamin was thrilled. At last he was reunited with his father. And he had a new mother—"Mother Sadie," as he and his sisters called her.

Next, the Army sent Benjamin's father to Alabama. He would be teaching military science tactics at the Tuskegee Institute, an all-black college.

Benjamin liked his new home in Tuskegee. He had his own bedroom and liked living in the country. He liked the friendly way the people in the South said hello when he walked down the street, even if they didn't know him.

But that was only on the college campus, where everybody else was black, too. The rest of Tuskegee didn't like black people, and they let him know it in all sorts of ways. There were signs everywhere he went that said "Whites Only." Sometimes the hatred even found its way onto the Tuskegee campus. Benjamin would never forget the night the Klan marched past his house.

When he was in seventh grade, his father was transferred again, and the family moved to Cleveland, Ohio. Benjamin's school was large and racially mixed. There were white, black,

Italian, and Polish students. Mother Sadie made sure that Benjamin studied hard. Even when he didn't want to, he read books every night because Mother Sadie said reading was important. Benjamin's father was equally strict. He wanted his children to do their very best.

All Benjamin's hard work paid off. He became an excellent student—except when it came to music. His parents insisted that he take piano lessons. But Benjamin couldn't understand why his teacher wouldn't teach him to play *fun* music, the exciting new kind called "jazz." He complained until finally his parents allowed him to stop taking lessons.

But if music didn't excite Benjamin, something else did. He discovered it by accident when he was almost fourteen. His parents were in Europe for the summer, and Benjamin was staying with his aunts and uncles in Washington. It was during this visit that his Uncle Ernest took him to see his first air show.

It was 1926. In those days, men called "barnstormers" traveled around the country in airplanes. They put on shows, doing tricks in their little planes. Afterward, they took passengers up for rides.

Uncle Ernest took Benjamin to a dirt field to watch the show. The sky was blue and crystal clear as he stood watching the brightly colored airplanes, turning loops in the air high above his head. The planes were made of wood and canvas. They had two sets of wings, one above the other. They weren't very sturdy compared with today's airplanes.

Benjamin couldn't forget the sight of those amazing machines, swooping and diving in the summer sky. When his father returned from Europe, he asked if he could visit the airfield again.

When they arrived at the field, his father realized that the boy was completely fascinated by these airplanes. He took five dollars from his pocket and bought a ticket for a ride. That was a great deal of money in 1926. But Benjamin's father saw something very special in his son's eyes that day. He had never before seen him so excited. And that ride changed Benjamin's life.

The airplane looked very frail as he climbed up to the cockpit. He had to wear goggles and a helmet because the cockpit was open. The airplane engine was very loud as it began to head down the runway. The wind blew hard in Benjamin's face, but he was thrilled when the tiny plane lifted off the ground.

In a few seconds they were high above the airfield. Benjamin looked down and saw his father, who looked like a tiny speck on the ground. Then the pilot made the airplane dive and swoop and somersault. It was a feeling like nothing Benjamin had ever experienced before. And one he would never forget.

A year later, Charles Lindbergh flew across the Atlantic Ocean alone. Benjamin followed the story of his flight excitedly. He wanted to be like Lindbergh. Somehow he felt certain that his own future would include flying.

Invisible Man

When he graduated from high school, Benjamin knew what he wanted to do: fly airplanes. But how? It was impossible for a black person to become a professional pilot. As he later wrote, "There weren't a lot of opportunities open to blacks when I came along and was trying to figure out what I was going to do with my life."

Finally Benjamin enrolled at Western Reserve University. But he wasn't really very interested in mathematics, the course of study he had chosen. He felt unhappy and confused. In his heart, he knew he was just killing time.

He considered moving to South America, where blacks were treated more fairly. He also thought about going to West Point, the college in New York State where Army officers are educated. Still, even if he was accepted there, he doubted that the Army would ever let a black man become a pilot.

But Colonel Davis hoped that his son would go to West Point anyway. He believed that blacks had an important role to play in the military. Benjamin admired his father and wanted to make him happy.

But even for a white student, it was very difficult to get admitted to West Point. A student had to have excellent grades. He had to be in very good physical condition. And—hardest of all—he needed to be nominated by a congressman.

There was almost no chance that a white congressman would nominate a black student. And there was only one black representative in Congress at that time—Oscar De Priest. Colonel Davis, who was the only black command grade officer in the entire Army, wrote to De Priest about his son.

Congressman De Priest wrote back that he would be glad to recommend Benjamin. But first he would have to move to Illinois, the state that Congressman De Priest represented.

Benjamin moved to Chicago, and in 1931 he was officially nominated to be a student at West Point. But before he could be admitted, he had to pass a very tough three-day examination. Unfortunately, he didn't study for it, and he failed.

This was common—many students failed it on their first try. But Benjamin was filled with shame. The hardest part was writing to his father about it. His father was so proud of him, and he had let his father down.

But his father didn't give up in disgust. Instead he encouraged his son to try again. Benjamin studied for months to be sure he would pass this time. And on his second try, he was accepted at West Point.

Benjamin had certainly made his father proud. Colonel Davis wrote, "Remember twelve million people [the black population of the United States] will be pulling for you. . . . your loving Dad."

Benjamin was just as proud of his father. He had risen through the ranks of the Army, fighting terrible prejudice every step of the way. "He had made life easier for me," Benjamin wrote. "Now it was my turn to make things better for those who would come after me. I was determined to succeed."

He had no idea how hard that was going to be.

Benjamin arrived at West Point in a bus full of other new students called *cadets*. The bus drove slowly past the huge stone buildings of

19

the campus. Benjamin was trying to see everything at once. He had never before been so excited. Soon he would be learning to be a professional officer, just like his father. He knew that the work would be difficult and challenging, but he wasn't worried. He was sure he would succeed.

New cadets like Benjamin were called "plebes." Plebes had to do anything an older student told them to do. The point of this practice was to teach them about following orders. "Break out in a sweat, mister," a student would bark. "Pull your chin in when you stand at attention!"

Plebes were not allowed to walk. They had to run everywhere they went. Plebes had to be ready to answer difficult questions at any time, even when they were trying to eat. Often plebes were made to stand at attention, very stiff and straight, for hours at a time. And there were hundreds of rules that had to be learned and obeyed.

Benjamin enjoyed the discipline. It was tough, but he knew that it would make him a stronger and better officer. Besides, all the other plebes were suffering, too.

Benjamin was very pleased at how well he seemed to be getting along at West Point. At first there was only one sign that he was being treated any differently from the others. Benjamin was living in a room that was big enough for two cadets—all by himself. Everyone else had a roommate. The commandant of cadets explained to Benjamin that he couldn't ask a white boy to room with a black boy.

Benjamin was shocked. But his problems were just beginning. Soon he heard that there was to be a meeting in the basement. He finished shining his shoes and polishing his brass buttons, and hurried downstairs. When he arrived, the meeting had already begun. As he approached, Benjamin heard one of his classmates asking, "What are we going to do about the nigger?"

Suddenly he realized something terrible: "The meeting was *about* me and not exactly *for* me." Just when he'd thought he was getting along so well at West Point, Benjamin had to face the truth. The other cadets were trying to get rid of him—not because he was a bad person, or had done something wrong. They wanted him out simply because he was the "wrong" color.

Soon their plan became all too clear. The white cadets had decided on a punishment called "silencing." Silencing meant that no student would talk to him, unless they had to in class. This punishment was used to get rid of those cadets who had cheated, or broken the code of honor—the set of rules every cadet must follow.

But Benjamin hadn't cheated. And he hadn't broken the code of honor. He was being silenced for only one reason—because he was black. The white cadets were certain that if they made him unhappy enough, he would resign.

What the cadets didn't understand was how determined Benjamin was to graduate and become an officer. They didn't count on his inner strength. Benjamin did *not* resign. And he never told his fellow cadets how miserably lonely and unhappy their bad treatment made him.

For the next four years, with a few brief exceptions, Benjamin did not have a single conversation with another cadet. Day in and day out, he endured the silence. He attended football games and other school events all by himself. No one would sit at the same table with him at meals. He couldn't even get his Red Cross lifesaving certificate because no one would be his buddy for the training. In a school full of students, Benjamin was completely alone. It was, Benjamin said later, like

"living as a prisoner in solitary confinement."
But he refused to accept defeat. *What they
don't realize,* he thought, *is that I am stubborn
enough to put up with their treatment to reach my
goal.*

Benjamin never mentioned any of this in
his letters to his parents. He held his head high
and refused to show his hurt to anyone. He felt
anger and betrayal and embarrassment, but he
also felt pity for the cadets who were trying to
get rid of him. *They are missing a great deal by not
knowing me,* he kept telling himself.

For a while, the only thing Benjamin had to
keep him company was a radio his mother had
sent him. Although it was against regulations to
have one, the radio was Benjamin's only friend.
He kept it hidden in his locker. When no one
else could hear, he would turn it on and listen
to voices from as far away as Boston and Chicago.

Two other things helped Benjamin survive
his long, lonely years at West Point. The first
was his belief in himself. His father had taught
him, "The impossible can be achieved." Benjamin was determined to achieve it—to keep
going, no matter what stood in his way.

Something else helped give Benjamin the
courage to keep going. During the Christmas

holiday in 1933, he met a beautiful woman at a New Year's Eve dance. She wasn't easy to forget—she had poured confetti down the back of his coat! In January, Benjamin wrote her a long letter. He didn't even know her first name, and had to address the envelope "Miss (?) Scott."

He soon learned her first name. Agatha Scott was a schoolteacher who lived with her parents in New Haven, Connecticut. She didn't smoke, didn't drink, and was friendly, popular, and artistic. And Benjamin was falling in love with her.

During his years at West Point, Agatha drove to visit him there nearly every Saturday. She, too, had to suffer through the silencing Benjamin lived with every day. In all her visits to West Point, she never once met another cadet. Still, Benjamin remembered later, "We were happy despite our isolation and did not need anyone else." Agatha's love and support helped give him the strength to survive those lonely years.

In 1936 it was finally time to graduate. Benjamin was now Second Lieutenant Benjamin Davis, Jr., of the United States Army. Despite the horrible treatment he had endured at West Point, he graduated thirty-fifth out of 276 cadets.

Benjamin had accomplished the nearly impossible. He was the first black man to graduate from West Point. It was an especially proud moment for his father. He hadn't been able to go to West Point; instead, he'd had to work his way up through the ranks of the Army, starting as an enlisted man.

Now, his son was a pioneer. All over the country, newspapers featured stories about him. A well-known black magazine put a picture of Benjamin on its cover. "Number One Graduate of the Nation," read the headline.

He had accomplished one goal. But the big one still remained. Benjamin was determined to fly.

Black Wings

When a cadet performed as well at West Point as Benjamin had, he was allowed to ask for any type of Army assignment he liked. There was never any question about what Benjamin wanted. He wanted to join the Army Air Corps and learn to fly.

But in 1936 the Army was still completely segregated. Black officers weren't allowed to lead white troops. And the Army knew that if it let Benjamin join the Air Corps, he would end up doing just that. So they denied his request. But Benjamin wasn't about to give up now. He'd triumphed over four years of silence at West Point, and he could triumph over the Army's stubbornness, too.

Benjamin married Agatha as soon as he graduated. He was soon sent to Fort Benning, Georgia. Later he went to Tuskegee Institute, the same place his father had worked. This was a very difficult time for Benjamin. He was there as an administrator of junior ROTC units, but his duties weren't challenging. He longed to prove himself, but there seemed to be no way.

Then, in 1940, at the age of sixty-three, Benjamin's father was promoted to the rank of brigadier general. He was put in command of two regiments. All the soldiers were black, but all the officers in charge were white—except, that is, for Benjamin's father. It was a great honor, and Benjamin was very pleased when his father requested that Benjamin serve as his aide.

Soon after he had joined his father, an amazing thing happened. The President of the United States, Franklin D. Roosevelt, decided that it was time to give blacks a bigger role in the military. If the United States got into the war then going on in Europe, Roosevelt knew that the all-white Army Air Corps would need many new pilots. He ordered the Army to create a flying group, called a *squadron*, that would be all black. It would train at Tuskegee, and these pilots became known as the Tuskegee Airmen.

Benjamin, who had been promoted to captain, was to be in command of this new squadron. At last he was going to fly!

But not everyone was happy about the new

black 99th Pursuit Squadron. Some blacks dis-approved of the "Tuskegee Experiment," as it was called. They argued that blacks should not be involved in any segregated activity—they thought that the Army should be *integrated*. Then blacks and whites could work side by side.

Benjamin agreed that segregation was evil, and should be ended. But he thought it was better to have an all-black Air Corps squadron than to have no place at all for blacks who wanted to fly. And he was certain that if war came, black soldiers would prove that they were as brave as white soldiers. After that, they would have to be treated as equals.

But before the 99th could prove itself, he and his men had to learn flying. For Benjamin, it was even more thrilling than he'd imagined. Takeoffs and landings were first. Then came loops and acrobatics. Flying in tight formation with other planes was harder. And hardest of all was night flying.

Month after month, Benjamin practiced until he had become a superb pilot. But none of it ever seemed like work to him. "For me," he said, "flying was a complete, unadulterated joy."

Then one bright Sunday morning the world changed. In the words of President

Franklin Roosevelt, "Yesterday, December 7, 1941—a date which will live in infamy—the United States of America was suddenly and deliberately attacked by naval and air forces of the Empire of Japan." The American naval base at Pearl Harbor was severely damaged, and many lives were lost.

The bombing of Pearl Harbor brought the United States into World War II, the largest and most terrible war in history. On one side were Japan, Germany, and Italy. On the other were the United States, Great Britain, the Soviet Union, and many smaller countries. It was a struggle to the death between freedom and dictatorship.

Germany was ruled by Nazis. The Nazis believed that Germans should rule the world. They believed that many other kinds of people, including Jewish people, should be killed.

While the Nazis were in power they forced Jews into concentration camps. Men, women, and even little children were herded together and killed like animals. The Nazis murdered six million Jews and many other people as well.

This was the enemy that Benjamin and his men would soon be fighting. He had been promoted to the rank of lieutenant colonel in May 1942 and was in charge of the entire 99th Pursuit Squadron. It included twenty-three pilots and many other men who took care of the airplanes.

On April 2, 1943, the 99th was at last ready to enter the war. As Benjamin boarded a train that would take them to New York, he kissed Agatha good-bye. He knew there was a chance that he would never see her again. He also knew that the performance of his men could affect the future of blacks in the military for many years to come. "Be proud of yourselves," Benjamin told his pilots. "Carry out the missions that are assigned you and set the stage for future recognition by America."

In New York they boarded a ship called the *Mariposa* that was headed for the war in Europe. Even Benjamin didn't know exactly where they were going. It was important to keep all troop movements secret from enemy spies.

Once at sea, Benjamin learned that they were headed for Northern Africa. World War II had started in Europe, but the fighting had spilled over into Africa. By the time the 99th arrived, the Germans and Italians were almost beaten there. But they still held a small island in the Mediterranean Sea called Pantelleria. It would be the job of the 99th to attack that island, to hit enemy positions with 500-pound bombs.

Their other job was to escort the bombers, protecting them from enemy fighters. Benjamin and his pilots liked this job better. It meant they would be involved in "dogfights," fierce battles between fighter aircraft.

On June 9, the pilots of the 99th Squadron had their first encounter with the enemy. Twelve of Benjamin's pilots were protecting a group of bombers. Suddenly, four airplanes attacked them. Eight of Benjamin's pilots stayed with the bombers. The other four went up to meet the German fighters—planes that were faster than theirs, with pilots who were far more experienced.

It was a terrifying moment, but the dogfight was over quickly. And when it was done, all four of the fighters from the 99th were unhurt. The Germans flew away quickly. One of their planes was damaged.

Benjamin was filled with pride. It was the first air combat for the 99th, and it had been a success.

Air War

July 2, 1943, was a memorable day for the men of the 99th Squadron.

The airfield was so dusty that the P-40s all had to take off at the same time to avoid getting lost in the dirt stirred up by the propellers. Twelve planes took off that morning, side by side.

Benjamin took the lead. They joined a group of two dozen B-25 bombers. Soon they were flying over the sparkling Mediterranean Sea on their way to Sicily, a large island between Africa and Italy.

As they flew, the pilots kept a sharp lookout for enemy planes. They knew the Germans would try to swoop down from the direction of the sun. The glare would make it hard for the Americans to fight back.

Suddenly Benjamin saw six enemy fighters overhead. The German planes dived toward the bombers, while six of Benjamin's P-40s soared up to meet them. Flying at hundreds of miles an hour, the Americans and Germans battled. Planes twisted and dived high in the air. The Americans tried desperately to get behind the enemy planes and fire before they were killed themselves.

One of the pilots of the 99th, Lieutenant Charles Hall, managed to bring his plane in behind a German fighter. The German plane tried to get away, but Hall squeezed the trigger and his machine guns blazed. Smoke began to billow from the German plane. It was hit!

But that same day, two members of the 99th died in air-to-air combat. The loss of these pilots hurt Benjamin terribly. He felt as though he had lost two brothers.

That afternoon a special visitor came to the dusty little airfield. It was Dwight D. Eisenhower, the general in charge of all the allied forces in Europe that were fighting the Germans and Italians. After the war, Eisenhower would become President of the United States. Eisenhower congratulated Benjamin and the men of the 99th on their first victory. It was exactly the sort of encouragement they needed after losing two pilots.

After the Germans and Italians were defeated in Sicily, the 99th moved its base there.

Now their pilots could attack the enemy in Italy itself.

In September 1943 the Army asked Benjamin to leave Sicily and return to the United States. The Army Air Corps had decided that the time had come for a much bigger all-black unit. And the clear choice to command it was Lieutenant Colonel Benjamin Davis.

But while he was at work forming the new unit, Benjamin discovered something that made him furious. Several Army officers had written a report claiming the 99th had performed poorly in combat. One of them said, "The Negro type has not the proper reflexes to make a first-class fighter pilot."

Benjamin knew that the best way to fight these lies was to let everyone in the Army know the truth. At several meetings he presented the facts about the 99th to Pentagon officers. And soon they began to believe him.

Fortunately, the 99th then put an end to the whole argument. In just two days at the beginning of 1944, the pilots of the 99th shot down twelve enemy fighters. This was especially impressive because at that time the Germans had better airplanes than the United States. Benjamin's men were finally beginning to get the recognition they deserved.

* * *

Organizing the new 332d Fighter Group proved to be a very difficult job. The base where he worked was called Selfridge, located just outside of Detroit, Michigan. The war was at its peak. In Europe, the Allies were fighting the Nazis. In the Pacific, they were fighting the Japanese. There was a constant shortage of men and supplies.

The 332d finally went to war at the end of January, 1944. It was stationed near Taranto, in Italy. The 99th Pursuit Squadron now became part of the 332d, reuniting Benjamin with old friends.

The 332d was a new unit, so at first they were given fairly safe work, patrolling along the coast. But Benjamin was pleased that they soon received another assignment. The pilots of the 332d were going to escort bombers flying into Germany—a very dangerous mission. And to carry it out, they were given a new type of aircraft—the P-47.

The P-47s were nicknamed "Jugs." They were not very pretty airplanes, but they were powerful, and the pilots liked them. For the first time, Benjamin and his pilots had a fighter that was just as good as the enemy planes.

Soon after getting the Jugs, the 332d was given the task of escorting a group of bombers going to Munich. This large German city was very heavily defended by antiaircraft guns and fighters.

As they flew toward Munich, Benjamin was at the head of his men. It was a long flight, taking several hours. The cockpits were small and uncomfortable. Fighter pilots had to stay very close to the big bombers all the way, requiring skilled and careful flying.

As they approached Munich, Benjamin spotted enemy fighters coming from high up on the right. He immediately radioed one of his two squadrons to turn toward the attack. But at that moment two German fighters came out of nowhere and went tearing through the bomber formation. Benjamin turned his P-47 sharply toward them, firing his machine guns. The German planes escaped—barely.

Meanwhile, the first squadron was in the midst of an intense fight with the main group of German planes. American and German fighters twisted and turned in the air high above the enemy city. Machine guns fired almost constantly. Antiaircraft fire exploded all around them. The noise was deafening—the battle was fierce. And when it was over, five enemy fighters had gone spiraling down in flames. The 332d hadn't lost a single plane.

When the tired pilots returned to their

base, they received a message from the commander of the bombers. "Your formation flying and escort work is the best we have ever seen," he wrote. Later, Benjamin was awarded the Distinguished Flying Cross for his courage and leadership.

By now the war was beginning to go badly for the Germans. Allied troops had landed on the coast of France in a huge invasion on June 6, 1944, called D-Day.

It was a very busy time for the 332d. Benjamin's fighters continued to escort bombers against German targets. They began flying a new plane called a "Mustang," the P-51. This was the best fighter of any air force in the war: it flew faster and higher and farther than any other. In their new Mustangs, the 332d scored victory after victory. In one eighteen-day period they destroyed thirty-nine enemy planes.

White American airmen had come to respect these black pilots very much. Every day compliments arrived by mail and telephone from those who had seen the 332d in action.

The war in Europe ended in May 1945. The Soviets had entered Berlin from the east; the Americans and British had smashed into Germany from the west. And Adolf Hitler, the leader of the Nazis, had killed himself in the ruins of his bunker.

Davis expected the 332d to be transferred to the Pacific for the fight against the Japanese, which was still going on. Instead, Benjamin was sent back to the United States to organize a new all-black unit, the 477th Bombardment Group.

But before the 477th could be brought into the fight against Japan, something new in the history of war happened. An American bomber took off carrying a single weapon—the atom bomb. It was dropped on the Japanese city of Hiroshima, creating the biggest explosion in history. Hiroshima was destroyed. Three days later, a second atom bomb was dropped on Nagasaki. The Japanese surrendered almost immediately.

As the war came to a close, Benjamin could look with pride on the record of his airmen. Black pilots had flown more than 15,000 missions. They had destroyed 261 enemy aircraft. And not one of the bombers they protected had been lost. These brave men had proved once and for all that black airmen could play an important role in the defense of their country. The "Tuskegee Experiment" was a success, thanks in large part to Benjamin's leadership.

He had proved that blacks could play an

important role as pilots. But he'd proved something else, too. Keeping blacks and whites in separate units had been very complicated and very expensive—a foolish waste of the Army's people and equipment. Would the U.S. military realize that it was time for them to end segregation?

The greatest war in history was over. But Benjamin still had a very important battle left to win.

"Benjamin O. Davis, Jr., American"

When Benjamin returned to the United States, he was reunited with the 332d Fighter Group at Lockbourne, a new base in Ohio. He was also reunited with his wife, Agatha. They had been separated for more than two years by the war, and it had been hard for both of them.

It was a time of many important changes—for Benjamin, and for his country. One of these occurred in 1947. The Army Air Corps separated from the Army to become the United States Air Force.

There were other changes, too. The war record of the 99th, the 332d, and other black units had begun to change the attitude of some white people in the military. Many now believed that blacks had earned the right to be treated as equals.

Finally, on July 26, 1948, President Harry S. Truman signed an executive order calling on all the armed forces to integrate black and white servicemen. From then on, there would be no more separate white units and black units. For the first time, black officers would be allowed to command white officers and men.

But outside the military, little had changed. Benjamin was a war hero. He had risked his life fighting for his country. Yet as he and Agatha drove to his next post in Alabama, they had to sleep in their car at night because hotels would not have them as guests. Signs saying "No Coloreds Allowed" were still to be seen.

At least in the armed forces conditions were beginning to improve. Official segregation—what Benjamin called "a cancer on the military"—was a thing of the past.

World War II was just the beginning of Benjamin's career in the military.

He was chosen to attend the Air War College, where he received advanced training. Afterward he worked as a planning officer for the Air Force Directorate of Operations, and later became Chief of the Fighter Branch. He supervised American fighters all over the world.

During this time, the Air Force started training its pilots to fly jets. Benjamin was thrilled at the opportunity to handle the powerful F-86 jet. He said, "I always felt a first surge of exhilaration when I climbed into the cockpit, another when I started the engine, another when I pushed the throttle forward for takeoff, and yet another when I was airborne."

No matter what position he held, Benjamin would never forget his first love—flying.

After his work at the Pentagon as Chief of the Fighter Branch, Benjamin went on to serve in Korea, Japan, the Philippines, Germany, and Taiwan.

Wherever they went, Benjamin and Agatha made it a point to meet the people of the country where they were traveling. They were known and respected by heads of governments, by soldiers of many different countries, and by their fellow Americans in the Air Force. Sadly, they often felt more comfortable in foreign countries, where racism was less of a problem, than they did at home in the United States.

But things were beginning to change in America. During the 1960s, Martin Luther King, Jr., began to be recognized as a leader among black Americans. Benjamin heard the famous speech King gave at the Lincoln Monument in Washington, D.C. When King said that he dreamed of an America where people would "not be judged by the color of their skin but by the content of their character," he could have been speaking straight to Benjamin. "Agatha and I were deeply moved by his words," he said, "and they still inspire us today."

Through the years, Benjamin sometimes had to work with the very men who had refused to speak to him while he was at West Point. But he had simply put that out of his mind. Besides, many had written him over the years, apologizing for what they had done.

He was especially pleased when his old classmates from West Point voted to honor him with the Benjamin F. Castle Award—a large silver platter with the words, "For Outstanding Service and Dedication to his Country and Alma Mater."

As 1970 approached, General Davis realized that the time had come for him to retire from the Air Force. By now he had three stars on his shoulder and a chest full of medals. A junior high school in California was named after him.

But once he retired, what then? A man like Benjamin wasn't about to sit on his porch in a rocking chair. And he didn't. First he was asked to be Safety Director for the City of Cleveland, Ohio. His job was to oversee the police and fire departments. From there, Benjamin was hired by the U.S. Department of Transportation. He worked to protect airlines from hijackers, and to make highways safer.

Finally, after thirty-seven and a half years in the military and a decade working in civilian life, Benjamin settled down to spend more time with Agatha. They visited many of the friends they had met throughout the world. And Benjamin started to write a book about his life. It was called *Benjamin O. Davis, Jr., American*.

The title was important to Benjamin. For him, being called an American was the greatest of all honors. The West Point motto he remembered well was, "Duty, Honor, and Country." He didn't want to be thought of as a black American, or a black general. He wanted to be thought of, first and foremost, as an *American*.

Today Benjamin Davis is retired and lives with Agatha in Arlington, Virginia.

Highlights in the Life of
General Benjamin O. Davis, Jr.

1912 Benjamin is born on December 18, in Washington, D.C.

1916 His mother dies after giving birth to his sister Elnora.

1917 His father is transferred overseas. He and his sisters go to live with their grandparents in Washington.

1919 On December 24, Benjamin's father marries Sadie Overton.

1920 His family moves to the Tuskegee Institute, and stays until 1924. It is during this time that the "night of the Klan" occurs.

1926 Benjamin takes his first ride in an airplane.

1931 On February 9, he receives a Congressional appointment to West Point. On April 7, he writes to tell his father he has failed the entrance examination.

1932 In March he passes the examination. On July 1, he arrives at West Point.

1936 After being silenced for four years at West Point, he graduates near the top of his class. He marries Agatha Scott.

1941 The Army decides to create the first all-black Air Corps unit. It is the 99th Pursuit Squadron, to be commanded by Benjamin.

1941 In July he begins to learn flying.

1943 In April the 99th leaves for the war in Europe. On July 2, the 99th scores its first air victories.

1944 He takes command of the 332d Fighter Group.

1948 On July 26, President Harry S. Truman orders the military to integrate.

1950 Benjamin becomes Chief of the Fighter Branch.

1953 He learns to fly jets.

1967 He is made Commander of the 13th Air Force.

1970 On February 1, Benjamin retires from the Air Force. He takes a job as Director of Public Safety for the City of Cleveland. Later, he becomes Director of Civil Aviation Security for the U.S. Department of Transportation.

1971 He is named Assistant Secretary of Transportation for Safety and Consumer Affairs.

1987 More than fifty years after graduating, he returns to West Point with Agatha to begin research for his book, *Benjamin O. Davis, Jr., American*.

1991 Benjamin's book is published.

Benjamin O. Davis, Jr., as a young officer with his wife, Agatha (right), and his father, General Benjamin Davis, Sr. (left).

General Davis, Sr., the first black man ever to become a general, decorates his son, Colonel Benjamin O. Davis, Jr.

Captain Benjamin Davis, Jr., learned to fly and led the 99th Pursuit Squadron, the first all-black Air Corps squadron, known as the Tuskegee Airmen.

The Tuskegee Airmen practice flight maneuvers using model planes at Tuskegee Field in Alabama during 1943.

Brigadier General Benjamin O. Davis, Sr., retired Army officer, looks at a photograph of his son after President Eisenhower named Benjamin, Jr., the first black Brigadier General in the Air Force in October, 1954.

U.S. Defense Secretary Dick Cheney and Gen. Colin L. Powell, Chairman of the Joint Chiefs of Staff, show off a Bart Simpson doll dressed in a desert camouflage uniform at a secret airbase in Saudi Arabia in February, 1991.

Craig Herndon/Washington Post

Powell and Davis, two great American generals, finally meet.

President George Bush reappoints General Colin Powell to a second two-year term as Chairman of the Joint Chiefs of Staff in May, 1991.

General Colin Powell meets with the Pentagon press on January 23, 1991, to assess Operation Desert Storm after the first week of the Persian Gulf War.

General Colin Powell meets with General H. Norman Schwarzkopf, Commander of allied forces in the Persian Gulf, at an airbase in Saudi Arabia in February, 1991, as the intense air war against Iraq continues.

Powell shakes hands with crew members of the battleship USS Wisconsin *in the Persian Gulf in September, 1990.*

Powell speaks at a ceremony in the Rose Garden of the White House after President Bush named him Chairman of the Joint Chiefs of Staff in August, 1989. Vice President Dan Quayle stands behind them. Powell became the youngest man and first black to hold this top military position.

General Powell receives some special guests in the Pentagon office in March, 1991   the Harlem Globetrotters.

General Colin Powell and his wife, Alma, attend a ceremony at Andrews Air Force Base welcoming the prisoners of war home from the Persian Gulf in March, 1991.

General Colin L. Powell
Beginnings

On May 5, 1937, a year after Benjamin Davis graduated from West Point, Colin Luther Powell was born.

His parents, Luther and Maud Ariel Powell, had come to the United States from Jamaica, an island in the Caribbean that then belonged to Great Britain. In many ways blacks in Jamaica were treated much more fairly than in the United States. But Colin's parents thought they would have a better life in America.

They believed that hard work would eventually pay off—if not for them, then for their children. They expected their children to take advantage of every opportunity, to work hard, and eventually to succeed. Colin's mother often told him to "make something of yourself."

They set a good example for their young son. Every day Colin saw his father come home late from his job as a shipping clerk—usually not until seven or eight o'clock at night. And when his mother got back from her work as a seamstress, she still had to care for Colin and the rest of the family.

For the first three years of his life, Colin lived in a section of New York City called Harlem. Then the family moved to a different neighborhood in the South Bronx. Almost everyone there had come from someplace else. Some were from Puerto Rico. Others were from Jamaica or other West Indies islands, like Colin's family. But most were Jews from countries all over the world. Growing up in the South Bronx, Colin never felt different because he was black. "I didn't know I was a minority because everybody there was a minority," he remembers.

Weekends were reserved for family and church. When the family got together, they often discussed current events. Colin was two years old when World War II started, and only eight when it ended. But he heard adults talking about it, and he was interested in all those battles far away. Sometimes he and other neighborhood children pretended they were soldiers, hiding between parked cars and using sticks for guns.

Other times Colin and his best friend Gene played stickball or raced their bicycles down the street. The Powells' neighborhood was almost like one big family—which meant it was difficult for Colin to get into any real trouble. Everyone in the area knew him, and knew his parents. Once, when he was eight, he tried to play hooky from school. He got away with it all day, but when he got tired and headed home he made a mistake—he arrived too early, before school let out. A neighbor who watched out for him while his parents were at work saw him and realized what Colin was up to.

That night Colin's parents gave him a good talking-to on the subject of honesty and education. And for some time afterward, one of his relatives took him to school to make sure he didn't try the same thing again. His parents were determined that their children grow up to have more opportunities than they had. They knew that the first step to success was education.

But Colin wasn't a very serious student. Nothing seemed to interest him very much. In fifth grade he was embarrassed to find himself in the "slow" class at Public School 39. Later, at

Morris High School, he "horsed around a lot," as he later admitted. Colin seldom earned grades better than a C. But everyone who knew him realized he wasn't "slow." He just hadn't found anything that truly excited him and made him want to learn.

Once he had graduated from high school, he knew it was time to think seriously about his future. At last he decided to attend the City College of New York. When it came to choosing the subject he would major in at CCNY, he was uncertain. He decided to try geology—geologists study rocks and how the earth was formed—mostly because it seemed fairly easy.

Then Colin made a decision that would change his life. As he strolled around campus, he noticed students wearing attractive uniforms with fancy decorations on them. I wouldn't mind wearing a uniform like that, Colin thought.

He found that these students were members of the Reserve Officer Training Corps, or ROTC. This is a program that gives college students some of the training they need to become Army officers. The students in the fine-looking uniforms belonged to the "Pershing Rifles," a fraternity that was part of ROTC. They were a precision drill team, which meant that they had to learn complicated marching steps.

He decided to join the ROTC. He didn't know it yet, but he had found the place he truly belonged.

As he went through college, Colin's grades were no better than they'd been in elementary and high school. He was still barely an average student in his geology courses. But he was a straight A student in his ROTC courses. The reason was simple. "When you find something you're good at, you tend to pursue it," Colin said.

Most of the other young men in the City College ROTC were Jewish; Colin was one of the few blacks. But that didn't hold him back—he soon became liked and respected by his ROTC classmates. He was chosen to be Commander of the Pershing Rifles and eventually became a cadet colonel—the highest rank in the ROTC.

Colin was learning to be a leader. Sometimes fellow students told him that they were thinking of leaving school. He knew that education was important, and he was almost always able to talk his friends into staying and getting their degrees.

In 1958 he graduated from college and

from the ROTC. He discussed his future with his parents and decided on the Army. "My parents expected that, like most young men going in the Army, I would serve for two years . . . and then come home and get a real job," Colin remembered later.

Fortunately, they were wrong.

Two Wars

After he graduated from college, Colin became Second Lieutenant Powell, U.S. Army. He was ordered to report for additional training at Fort Benning, Georgia, where he was to take the Infantry Officer's Training Course, which would teach him to command soldiers. He would also attend the Airborne and Ranger School, where soldiers were taught to parachute and to fight in the jungle. Colin knew it would be very tough training. He would be able to fight barehanded, and to jump from an airplane and parachute to the ground. By the time he was through, he would learn to survive in the woods without food.

Ranger training was just as difficult as he had thought it would be. Colin and his fellow lieutenants were sent out alone into the wilderness to survive as best they could.

As Colin walked through the dense woods of Georgia, he kept thinking how different all this was from the streets of New York. Here he had to climb down steep cliffs on ropes. He had to wade through swamps, holding his rifle over his head. It rained often, turning the ground to mud. Then at night, still soaking wet, he shivered in his sleeping bag. When he got hungry he had to find roots or leaves that were safe to eat, or catch a small animal he could cook.

Sometimes Colin saw snakes slithering toward him, but he didn't mind. Snakes were one of the things he had been taught he could eat in the wilderness!

At other times Colin trained with young officers like himself. Because he was tall and strongly built, he was usually given the job of carrying a heavy .30-caliber machine gun in addition to his regular backpack. At night he and the others crouched in the darkness beneath their ponchos, wondering what it would be like if they really were in a war and not just training.

It was hard work, but he began to realize that he liked it. He didn't exactly enjoy being cold and tired and dirty, but he did like being with his fellow soldiers, doing difficult jobs. He got along well with everyone. Often it was Colin who encouraged his friends when they were weary.

Colin experienced no problems with other soldiers because of his race. Things had definitely changed since Benjamin Davis had been stationed in the South. But off the Army post, segregation still ruled. Laws in southern states did not allow blacks to enter restaurants or hotels where whites went. Colin would have liked to get involved with the civil rights movement led by Martin Luther King, Jr., but Army officers were required to stay out of politics. He decided that if he wanted to help his fellow blacks, he would have to do it inside the Army.

Colin's first real assignment came in October 1958, when he was sent to Germany to command a platoon, a group of about a dozen men. American troops were in Germany to protect Europe from the Soviet Union.

The United States and the Soviet Union had been allies in World War II. But when the war was over, the Soviets began trying to take over other countries. The Soviets were ruled by the Communist Party. Communists believe, among other things, that people's lives should be completely controlled by the government.

The Americans and the Soviets were enemies for a very long time. The two countries never had a real war, but they prepared for one by stocking up on weapons. This era of competition and bad relations was called the "Cold War."

Soon after arriving in Germany, Colin was promoted to first lieutenant. Then, in 1960, he was sent back to the United States, to Fort Devins, Massachusetts.

While he was there, one of his friends arranged a blind date for him. Colin was a little nervous. He'd never even seen this woman. What if he didn't like her? Or worse yet, what if she didn't like him?

As it turned out, Alma Vivian Johnson and Colin liked each other very much. Alma was the daughter of a high school principal from Birmingham, Alabama. She was working on her master's degree at Emerson College in Boston. She hoped to become a speech pathologist, helping people learn to speak more clearly. But now her plans—and Colin's—changed. On August 24, 1962, they were married.

A few months later, Colin, who was now Captain Powell, received new orders. He was to go to Fort Bragg in North Carolina for a month of special training. His training would prepare him for a country that almost no one had even heard of in those days. When he told his parents he was being shipped to Vietnam, they had to look it up in an atlas to see where it was. It turned out to be thousands of miles away across the Pacific Ocean.

Colin was headed toward a foreign country and a very complicated war. South Vietnam was an ally of the United States. The Viet Cong was a group of revolutionaries trying to overthrow the government there. They were being helped by North Vietnam, which was Communist. American involvement in the war grew slowly over many years. The first few American troops arrived in 1961; by 1969 there were almost 550,000.

The American people began to disagree about the war. Many Americans believed that the Vietnamese people should solve their own problems. Others thought the United States should help the South Vietnamese defeat the Viet Cong. But as time went on, more and more Americans wanted to get out of Vietnam.

For the soldiers fighting the war, life was very difficult. Many people in South Vietnam were secretly on the side of the Viet Cong. It was often impossible for American soldiers to tell who was an enemy and who was a friend.

There were political problems, too. The government of the United States felt it should not use all its power in the war. It didn't want to invade North Vietnam because the Soviets and the Chinese were allies of the North. American leaders feared that an invasion might lead to a much bigger war between the United States and the whole Communist world.

This was a very important lesson for Colin. He would always believe that the United States lost the war in Vietnam because it refused to use all its power.

On this first trip to Vietnam, though, Colin wasn't worried about these issues. His job was to train the South Vietnamese military. He went out into the jungles and fields with their troops and tried to teach them what he knew about warfare.

Colin and the South Vietnamese went on patrol, walking single file through the wet rice paddies. Their boots got soggy and muddy. Mosquitoes swarmed around them, and leeches crawled onto their legs and sucked their blood. Sometimes Colin was so hot and tired he felt he simply could not go on with his work.

But no matter how tired they were, Colin and his men always had to be prepared for a fight. They kept their rifles ready at all times. As they walked, they constantly watched the jungle all around them for any sign of enemy soldiers.

A machine gun might suddenly start blazing away from the jungle, and Colin would dive to the ground. He and his men would lie flat in the mud, trying to keep the enemy from seeing them. Other times the enemy fired cannons and mortars, and Colin had to lie there while gigantic explosions went off all around him.

The Viet Cong had many tricks. They hid booby traps and mines that exploded when they were stepped on. They dug pits in the ground and covered them with branches, so that soldiers walking over them fell in. And there were "punji" sticks, pieces of wood or bamboo carved to a razor-sharp edge and hidden inside holes in the ground—waiting for an American soldier to step on them.

One day while on patrol Colin was wading through the muddy water of a rice paddy. As he walked, he carefully eyed the area for signs of the enemy. His men splashed through the water with him. Sometimes they stumbled into underwater holes and had to struggle to keep their rifles out of the water.

Colin was wading when he felt his foot come down on something hidden just below the murky surface of the water. He tried to pull back, but it was too late. An instant later, he felt a sharp stab of pain as the bamboo cut through the leather of his boot. He had stepped on a punji stick!

It was extremely painful, but he knew he

had a job to do. His unit had to arrive at a certain location in time to help another group of men. Despite the pain, Colin kept going and completed his task. Later he was awarded a Bronze Star for bravery.

Sometimes Colin was out in the jungle for weeks at a time. It was while he was on one of these trips that Alma gave birth to their first child—a boy named Michael. Two weeks passed before anyone could give Colin the message that he had become a father.

At the end of 1963, Colin returned home from Vietnam. He was very glad to be with Alma. And he was very proud to see his strong baby boy—who would soon be joined by two daughters. But while he was away fighting one war in Vietnam, another kind of war had broken out at home.

Alma had stayed with her parents in Birmingham, Alabama, while Colin was in Vietnam. And 1963 was not a good year in Birmingham. The civil rights movement had started some years before. Led by Martin Luther King, Jr., and others like him, blacks had finally begun to demand the freedom that should have been theirs all along. Through nonviolent resistance, they were challenging the whole idea of segregation in the South.

But the white racists were fighting back violently. Many churches with black congregations were bombed. Civil rights workers, black and white alike, were murdered by the Ku Klux Klan and other racist organizations. When blacks tried to go into "whites only" restaurants or attend all-white schools, they were often savagely beaten. And in most cases the white police did nothing to protect them. The sheriff in Birmingham, a man named Bull Connor, turned vicious attack dogs loose on civil rights protesters.

This was the war that Alma had lived through, while her husband was fighting for his country thousands of miles away. Now Colin could see firsthand what he'd only heard about in Vietnam.

For the next several years, he was stationed at Fort Benning, Georgia. He was an instructor in some courses, and a student in others. Treatment of blacks in the Army had improved, but off the post it was still the same old story. Once, while Colin was driving in nearby Columbus, he got hungry and stopped for a hamburger. He pulled into a place called Buck's Barbecue. The waitress asked him if he was Puerto Rican or perhaps a student from an African nation. When he said no, she knew he was an American black. She ordered him to leave the dining room and go around to the back door of the kitchen.

Colin had no choice but to do as he was told. At that time, the law was against him. But a few months later the Civil Rights Act was passed—a law making segregation illegal. Soon afterward, Colin returned to Buck's Barbecue. This time the law was on his side. The waitress still didn't like waiting on a black man, but she did it. Today, many years later, the street in Columbus where Buck's Barbecue once stood is called Martin Luther King Avenue.

In the summer of 1967, Colin enrolled in the Command and General Staff College at Fort Leavenworth, Kansas. He knew this was an important point in his career. He was haunted by his earlier lazy attitude toward school. It had taken him a while, but he had discovered how important education could be to his career in the Army.

Colin went to see his commanding officer and asked if he could take some extra classes at a local college. The officer looked over his academic record and shook his head. "Your grades aren't good enough," he said.

Colin knew this was true, but he was angry anyway. It was time to show everyone, including himself, just what he could accomplish.

From that moment on, Colin studied harder than he ever had before.

And it paid off. There were 1,244 students graduating from the Staff College that year. Colin Powell, once a C student, was now ranked second in the class!

Crash Landing!

As soon as he completed the course at Leavenworth, Colin was sent back to Vietnam. He was now a major, and became the executive officer of a battalion in the Americal Division. Colin was back in "the boonies"—what soldiers called the jungles of Vietnam—once again fighting the war that seemed to go on forever. By now, there were half a million American soldiers there.

Not long after that, an article appeared in the Army newspaper about the top graduates from the Staff College. The commanding officer of the Americal Division was reading it when he recognized a name—Colin Powell. The officer was furious. He called in his aides and shouted, "I've got the number two Leavenworth graduate in my division, and he's stuck in the boonies? I want him on my staff!"

Colin was quickly called in from the field and put to work as operations chief for the division. His hard work at Staff College had earned him an important assignment. It should have been a safer assignment, too—but it didn't work out that way. For it was during this time that Colin became a hero by risking his life to save others.

He was flying in a helicopter along with his commander and some other soldiers. The chopper—as a helicopter is often called—was just above the trees. Hills rose on either side as the pilot searched for the landing zone—a tiny clearing in the jungles of Vietnam. Then he spotted it.

Colin looked out through the open side door. He could see that there would be barely enough room for the chopper to land. As it headed down, he realized something was wrong. The pilot was losing control of his craft!

Suddenly the helicopter slid sideways. Colin watched in horror as the rotor blade slammed into a tree. It stopped instantly. The chopper fell like rock.

Remembering his training, he bent over and put his hands under his knees. Seconds later the helicopter crashed to earth. Colin instantly tore off his seat belt and jumped from the crippled aircraft. Several feet away, he turned to look back. The other men should have been behind him. But they were trapped inside.

Then he saw smoke beginning to pour from the helicopter. At any moment it could burst into flames, killing his fellow soldiers. And if he went back to help them, he could be caught in the fire himself.

It was a grim moment of decision, but Colin did not hesitate. He raced back to the chopper. He tried to reach inside and pull his commander out, but wreckage blocked his way. He grabbed a piece of steel and twisted with all his might. It came loose!

Colin reached in and began freeing the men. One by one they crawled out of the shattered helicopter. At last only the pilot was left. Colin saw that his helmet had become stuck on a broken piece of the controls. He had to twist the helmet to free it. Finally Colin managed to lift the unconscious man from the aircraft.

Other choppers began to land nearby. They picked up the wounded men and rushed them to hospitals. When all his fellow officers were safe, Colin climbed on board the last helicopter.

He was later awarded the Soldier's Medal for his bravery that day. The citation said, "With complete disregard for his own safety,

and while injured himself, Major Powell returned several times to the smoldering aircraft
which was in danger of bursting into flames. In
one instance he had to break away part of the
wreckage to get to a trapped individual.
Through his efforts all personnel were saved."

"It wasn't anything too heroic," Colin re-
marked years later. But the men whose lives he
saved that day would probably disagree.

New Battles

When Colin came home from Vietnam, there were no parades to welcome him back. He returned to a country that had been deeply divided by the war. Many people who opposed it blamed the soldiers themselves for it. There were many angry demonstrations.

Colin had already learned that no war should be fought halfway. What he saw at home convinced him of something else: The United States should never fight a war unless the American people supported it. He would always remember that.

The value of education had never seemed so important to him. At the age of 32, he decided to go back to school. He enrolled at a college in Washington, D.C., and got an advanced degree in business.

Then something unexpected happened— something that would greatly affect Colin's future. The White House had a program that recruited bright men and women from many different fields to become White House Fellows. They were to be given special jobs in the government so that they could learn how it really works. Fifteen hundred people applied—and Colin was one of the seventeen accepted.

He was assigned to work at the Office of Management and Budget, located next to the White House. Colin quickly impressed his new bosses there.

But not for long. The Army wanted him back. He was asked to go to Korea and take over a problem battalion of American soldiers stationed there. Some of the soldiers were using drugs, and there were conflicts between black troops and white. With his usual speed, Colin began taking care of the matter. He threw the drug users out or had them put in jail. He made the rest of his men run four miles every morning, and worked them harder every day. By the time he was done with them, the men were too tired to get into trouble. Within a few months the white and black soldiers were getting along just fine.

Colin returned to the United States, where he attended the National War College to learn more about the history of war. He was then given a variety of jobs. Some were for the

Army; others were for the Department of Defense, which controls all the military services. It was the beginning of a battle between the two groups. Each wanted Colin, who was now a colonel, for themselves. He soon became a Special Assistant to the Deputy Secretary of Defense.

In July 1983 he became the Senior Military Assistant to Caspar Weinberger, the Secretary of Defense. Weinberger had worked with Colin before and had been very impressed with him. The two men grew to be close friends.

Colin was quickly promoted to brigadier general and then to major general. In his new position in the Defense Department, he had to deal with many important matters.

A group of American Marines had been sent to Lebanon, where many different armed groups were fighting one another. The U.S. government hoped it could restore order with a force of peacekeeping troops. But one day a terrorist drove a truck loaded with dynamite into the Marines' barracks. Two hundred and forty-one Marines were killed. The Pentagon was stunned.

Only two days after the bombing of the Marines in Lebanon, American troops invaded the tiny Caribbean island nation of Grenada.

Grenada was controlled by a Communist government. The United States believed that other Communist powers would use the island as an anti-American base.

The attack was planned hurriedly, and did not go well. The Communists fought back harder than anyone had expected. The United States won, but there were losses.

After these two unfortunate incidents the Army called Colin back. They had let the politicians have him long enough. They wanted him to take over the 5th Corps in Germany. The job would involve commanding a force of 75,000 men, and it meant a great deal of responsibility.

It was Colin's dream come true. He had always wanted to be in charge of a large force of men. He would be on his own, far from politics, doing what he did best.

He was, he said, "probably the happiest general in the world."

Chairman of the Joint Chiefs of Staff

Six months after Colin got his dream job, he received an important phone call. The White House wanted him back to help the new National Security Advisor, Frank Carlucci, who was the President's closest consultant on foreign policy.

Colin refused. "No way," he said. Commanding the 5th Corps was the best job he'd ever had. He was happy back in the Army and away from politics. Things were simpler. Besides, Alma had already joined him in Germany. She had just barely settled into their new home.

Carlucci called a second time, asking Colin to come back to Washington. Again, Colin flatly refused. A third time Carlucci called back. He said, "Colin, I wouldn't ask you to give up this command if I didn't need you. The Commander-in-Chief needs you."

By the Commander-in-Chief, Carlucci

meant President Ronald Reagan. Colin knew he could still refuse, but he hated to turn down the President of the United States. "If he really wants me," Colin said, "then I have to do it."

When the phone rang the next day, Colin heard a very familiar voice. "I know you've been looking forward to this command," President Reagan said. "But we need you here."

"Mr. President," Colin replied, "I'm a soldier, and if I can help, I'll come." Colin gave up his command and returned to Washington with Alma.

Soon after that, he received some shocking news. His only son Michael, who was now an Army officer himself, had been terribly injured in a jeep accident. The doctors weren't sure he would live. And even if he lived, they thought he would never be able to walk again.

Colin rushed to his son's hospital room. He could see that Michael was a mass of shattered bones. Tubes were stuck into his arms and down his throat. Bandages covered his whole body.

Colin was more worried than he had ever been in his life. Nothing was as frightening to him as the thought of his son dying. But he knew he must not let Michael see his fear.

"You'll make it," Colin promised his son. "You want to make it, so you *will* make it!"

After surgery, Michael went to stay with Colin and Alma at their home near the Pentagon. For weeks, therapists came and went, helping Michael conquer his injuries. As the weeks became months, Colin kept reassuring his son that he would get better.

And he did. Sixteen months later, Michael married his college sweetheart. He had to use a cane to walk down the aisle of the church, but just as Colin had promised, he *was* walking.

After a year, Frank Carlucci became Secretary of Defense. Everyone wondered who would take over the extremely important job of National Security Advisor to the President. But when the members of the President's staff sat down to discuss the matter, only one name was mentioned: Colin Powell. Immediately President Reagan said, "I think that's a great idea."

Colin was now at the very center of power in Washington. Every morning he got up early and read a thick pile of reports from all around the world. Some were from newspapers. Others were from American secret agents, or spy satellites. Many were from military personnel all around the world.

Then he went in to the President's office

and discussed the information that affected American security with President Reagan.

During this time Colin also met two very dangerous men who were to play a large part in his life. The first was Manuel Noriega. He was the leader of Panama, a small country in Central America. A dictator, Noriega was later accused of smuggling drugs into the United States. Colin tried to get Noriega to give up power peacefully, but without result.

The other man, also a dictator, was even more dangerous. He was Saddam Hussein, the leader of Iraq. He had invaded the neighboring country of Iran. The United States considered Iran an enemy, so they supported Saddam Hussein during this long war. But Colin knew that Saddam was very dangerous.

In 1989 President Reagan left office after two terms. George Bush, who had been Reagan's Vice President, had been elected the new President of the United States. President Bush liked and respected Colin, but he wanted someone he had chosen himself as National Security Advisor.

Once he had left the White House, Colin got two job offers. The first was from his beloved Army. They wanted him back. They had a very important job for him as Commander of Forces Command in Georgia—he would be a four-star general.

The other offer was from a publishing agent in New York. He told Colin he could make at least a million dollars going around the country giving speeches. Perhaps he could also write a book.

The idea of telling his story was very appealing to Colin. He had already risen far higher than he ever expected he would. He was famous and well-liked—now he could also be rich.

Colin took a piece of paper and on one side he wrote, "Reasons to stay in the Army." On the other side he wrote, "Reasons to Leave." He put down everything he could think of, but when he looked at it, he realized he had a long list of reasons to stay in the Army. The only reason to leave was "money."

He called up Army headquarters, and took the assignment in Georgia.

But Colin wasn't allowed to stay in his new job very long. The Chairman of the Joint Chiefs of Staff, Admiral William Crowe, was about to retire. He was the highest military officer in the country. He worked with the Chiefs of the Army, Air Force, Navy, Marine Corps, and

Coast Guard. And he was the President's most important military advisor.

There were a number of men who were considered to be good candidates for Chairman. But in the end, once again, the President's choice was obvious. Colin Powell was the best man for the job. At 52, he became the youngest officer, and the first black man, ever to serve as Chairman.

Colin's new job wasn't easy. Two days after he was chosen, Panamanian soldiers attempted to overthrow Manuel Noriega. They begged for help from the United States, but no plans had been made for getting involved. Colin had to refuse, and the attempt failed. Noriega remained in power.

Colin was criticized for not being prepared to deal with the problem in Panama. He was determined to be ready the next time. He sat down with his generals and went to work.

When President Bush approved his new plan, Colin and his generals acted swiftly, yet carefully. He wanted to be as cautious as he could about using troops. "But when it's clear we're going to use them, let's use them," he said decisively.

Helicopters began landing in Panama. The Panamanian army resisted. Most of its troops were still loyal to Noriega. But the 26,000 American soldiers Colin had sent overwhelmed them. Noriega barely escaped, and hid in the embassy of the Vatican. Embassies may not be entered by troops, so the Americans waited outside for Noriega to surrender.

Then they tried a very clever plan. They set up loudspeakers and blasted the embassy with rock music, expecting it to drive the dictator crazy. And it must have, for a few days later Noriega surrendered. He was arrested on drug charges and taken to jail in the United States.

Operation Just Cause, as the mission was called, had been a success, thanks in large part to the planning and boldness of Colin Powell.

Operation Desert Storm

Colin was the most powerful black man in the history of the United States. The same military that had treated Benjamin Davis as an unwanted intruder was now under Colin's control.

As Chairman of the Joint Chiefs of Staff, Colin was given an official residence—a beautiful old house on a hill at Fort Myer, Virginia. It was near the Potomac River, and Colin could sit with Alma and look across at the nation's capital. He could see the tall needle of the Washington Monument and the white pillars of the Lincoln Memorial.

Colin's son Michael now worked at the Pentagon. His daughter Linda was an actress in New York, and his youngest daughter, Annemarie, was a college student. He had a baby grandson named Jeffrey—Michael's son. He spent as much time as he could with his family, despite his busy schedule. Work didn't leave him many hours for his favorite hobby—fixing up old cars. Besides, he knew that old junkers wouldn't look quite right in the yard of the Chairman's official residence.

Colin had come a long way. He'd survived a war in Vietnam. He'd been involved in a number of military conflicts. He'd worked for three Presidents and was one of the best-liked and most admired people in the government.

But the biggest test of his life was yet to come.

In the summer of 1990, Colin began getting reports about a man he had dealt with before. Saddam Hussein, the dictator of Iraq, was threatening to invade his tiny neighbor, Kuwait. Despite its size, Kuwait was a very wealthy country because of its vast supplies of oil.

No one believed Saddam Hussein would actually invade. They thought he was just trying to scare the Kuwaitis into giving him more money.

On the evening of August 2, Colin received word that the Iraqi army had crossed the border into Kuwait. The leader of Kuwait had barely escaped. The main Kuwaiti radio station broadcast a desperate cry for help. "Hurry to our aid!" it called. Then it went dead.

The Pentagon erupted into frenzied activity. There were many unanswered questions. What if the Iraqis kept going? South of Kuwait was the large desert kingdom of Saudi Arabia. It was an ally of the United States and possessed much of the world's oil. Saudi Arabia was weak. If the Iraqis continued their march, there was no chance that the Saudi military would be able to stop them.

Colin spent the next few days in long meetings with the President and his aides. President Bush began talking to U.S. allies, getting their reactions to the crisis.

Colin had many things to consider. He knew that it would be almost impossible to get enough U.S. troops to Saudi Arabia in time to stop Saddam. Still, he said, the President should "draw a line in the sand." Saddam, Powell said, had to be told that "If he attacks Saudi Arabia, he attacks the United States."

Colin began to plan the largest, fastest movement of American troops in history. All over the world, military bases went on alert. Cargo planes filled with everything from tanks to food and medicine flew to Saudi Arabia. Tens of thousands of soldiers and Marines began to arrive. Hundreds of U.S. warplanes began crossing the ocean, refueling in midair and flying on at more than a thousand miles an hour.

Fifty warships turned in midsea and steamed at full speed for the Persian Gulf, which borders Kuwait. There were destroyers, battleships, and aircraft carriers. Many other nations contributed to the effort, too. Some sent troops, others sent supplies or money.

As forces poured into Saudi Arabia, Colin met with the President again. The two men discussed how they could force the Iraqis to back away from Saudi Arabia and give up Kuwait. Colin remembered every lesson he had learned, from Vietnam to Panama. He knew they couldn't do things halfway. "Don't count on the easy ways," he advised President Bush. If the United States was going to go to war against Saddam, he believed, then it had to go all out.

As troops and weapons arrived in Saudi Arabia, Saddam Hussein sent his own troops into Kuwait. The show of American power had kept him from invading Saudi Arabia. But he was preparing to fight for Kuwait. He was surrounding the invaded country with mine fields, barbed wire, and hidden tanks.

As the crisis grew more intense, Colin flew to Saudi Arabia to talk with General Norman Schwarzkopf, the American commander on the scene. They discussed plans for pushing Saddam out of Kuwait. But the generals were worried. If U.S. forces attacked the Iraqis, the number of American deaths could be very, very high. He and General Schwarzkopf agreed that if they had to fight, they were determined to win quickly and decisively. That was the best way to save American lives.

While Colin was in Saudi Arabia, he visited many American troops. Talking with ordinary soldiers was one of the things he liked best about this job. Wherever he went, he joked with them and posed for pictures. He listened to their complaints and tried to help. And everywhere he went, he assured his troops that this would not be another long drawn-out war like Vietnam. This time, he promised, "If we go in, we go in to win, not to fool around."

Back in the United States people were debating about what to do in Kuwait. Some argued that America was only getting involved because Kuwait had so much oil. Others were afraid that the war against Iraq would drag on for a long time. Thousands of American soldiers could be killed, they warned. They argued that there were other ways to resist Saddam without using force. Already Iraq was suffering because most of the world refused to buy its oil or to send it anything but medical supplies.

The United Nations had been involved in the Gulf Crisis almost from the start. The United Nations is an organization of more than 150 countries that tries to find peaceful solutions to world problems. Now the United Nations and the American President gave Iraq a deadline: be out of Kuwait by January 15, 1991, or be driven out.

Saddam ignored the warning. Hours after the deadline, "Operation Desert Storm" began. Jets shot into the sky from Saudi airfields. Giant B-52 bombers took off from faraway bases. Cruise missiles were fired from battleships and submarines. Navy jets roared off the decks of aircraft carriers.

The attack was like a hammer blow. The Iraqis reeled. And it continued, on and on, twenty-four hours a day. To Colin's great relief, very few Americans were being killed or injured.

Colin felt that part of his job was to help explain the war to the American people. He knew it was important for them to support their military. He went on television to explain the strategy. While millions of people all around the world watched, he looked straight into the camera. His voice was steady and his eyes glinted. The plan to defeat the Iraqi army was simple, Colin explained. "First we're going to cut it off, and then we are going to kill it."

Colin met again with the President and suggested giving Saddam one last deadline. Tell him he must leave Kuwait completely and totally by noon Saturday, Colin advised. The President followed his instructions, but the Iraqis refused to leave. One hour after noon, President Bush appeared on television, saying he regretted Saddam's decision.

That was the signal for General Schwarzkopf. Five hundred thousand U.S. and allied troops attacked on February 23. About the same number of Iraqi soldiers faced them, dug in behind very strong defenses.

Just one hundred hours later, on February 27, Iraqi troops were surrendering faster than the Americans could count them.

The victory was complete. Very few U.S. soldiers had been killed. But it was estimated that as many as 100,000 Iraqis had died.

Colin was sad that the war had to take place. But he was very pleased that it had been so effective. Now, when people thought of the U.S. military they would remember the American victory in Iraq. American soldiers would be respected. All around the country people welcomed the soldiers home with parties and parades.

Colin was hailed as a hero, too. Many people thought he might someday become the first black President of the United States.

For Colin, though, this victory was enough. He was proud of the part he had played. But he was far prouder of his brave troops—men and women, black and white, from every part of the nation. "What they did for freedom," he said with pride, "will never, never be forgotten."

Operation Desert Storm was well under way on February 6, when a new play opened in Washington, D.C. That was a busy time for General Colin Powell, but he managed to slip away to the theater to see the first performance.

It wasn't just any play. "Black Eagles" was the story of the Tuskegee Airmen and their brilliant feats during World War II. In the last scene of the play, the black airmen get together for a reunion in 1989. On stage they have a toast, cheering Colin Powell's rise to the top of the U.S. military.

Watching this scene, the audience stood and applauded wildly. They knew Colin was in the theater, and they wanted to express their appreciation for his leadership during Operation Desert Storm.

Also applauding was another famous general. Benjamin Davis was there that night, watching his own story unfold on the stage. Twenty-five of the Tuskegee Airmen were there as well.

In the theater lobby, Colin and Benjamin spoke together—of the past, of the future, of the war just then unfolding. Colin knew he owed a large debt of gratitude to the brave black pioneers before him. Without men like Benjamin Davis he would probably never have gone so far.

"I've known about the Tuskegee Airmen all my life," Colin said. "They have been part of my whole military life and career."

The real stars that night weren't on the stage.

General Colin Powell's Rules

As he grew older and gained more experience, Colin realized there were certain ideas that guided his behavior. Here are his thirteen rules to live by:

1. It isn't as bad as you think. It will look better in the morning.

2. Get mad, then get over it.

3. Avoid having your ego so close to your position that when your position falls, your ego goes with it.

4. It can be done!

5. Be careful what you choose. You may get it.

6. Don't let adverse facts stand in the way of a good decision.

7. You can't make someone else's choices. You shouldn't let someone else make yours.

8. Check small things.

9. Share credit.

10. Remain calm. Be kind.

11. Have a vision. Be demanding.

12. Don't take counsel of your fears or nay-sayers.

13. Perpetual optimism is a force multiplier. (In the military, one always looks for ways to increase or multiply one's forces.)

Highlights in the Life of
General Colin L. Powell

1937 Colin is born on May 5, in Harlem.

1940 His family moves to the South Bronx.

1954 He enters the ROTC program at the City College of New York.

1958 Colin graduates with a degree in geology and the rank of second lieutenant. From June to October he takes Ranger and Airborne training in Georgia.

1959 He gets his first command—a platoon in Germany.

1962 On August 24, he marries Alma Johnson. In December he is sent to Vietnam for the first time and is injured.

1963 Colin returns from Vietnam to learn that Alma has been surrounded by the racial strife of the early 1960's.

1967 He is sent to the Staff College at Fort Leavenworth.

1968 He goes back to Vietnam, where he earns the Soldier's Medal for rescuing men from a downed helicopter.

1972 Colin becomes a White House Fellow, his first brush with politics.

1973 He is sent to Korea to straighten out a battalion plagued with drug and race problems.

1976 He attends the National War College and takes command of an airborne brigade in Kentucky.

1977 He becomes Special Assistant to the deputy Secretary of Defense.

1983 Colin is named Senior Military Assistant to the Secretary of Defense.

1986 He is made commanding general of the 5th Corps in Germany.

1987 He is called back to the White House to become Deputy Advisor and later National Security Advisor to the President.

1989 He becomes Commander-in-Chief, Forces Command. In October, Colin becomes the nation's highest ranking military officer, the Chairman of the Joint

Chiefs of Staff. In December, U.S. forces invade Panama.

1990 He is in charge at the Pentagon in August, when Iraqi forces under the command of Saddam Hussein invade Kuwait.

1991 Colin helps plan the attack against Iraq. In mid-January, U.S. ground forces attack. One hundred hours later, Iraqi troops are beaten.

In May, acting four months early, President Bush reappoints Colin to a second two-year term as Chairman of the Joint Chiefs of Staff.